# Anorexia Nervosa: When Food Is the Enemy

# Anorexia Nervosa: When Food Is the Enemy

Erica Smith

The Rosen Publishing Group/New York

The Teen Health Library of Eating Disorder Prevention

*for Cyndy*
*wise sage*

Thanks to Jane Kelly Kosek, Michele Drohan, and Caroline Levchuck of the Rosen Publishing Group, whose editorial skill and knowledge of eating disorders have been invaluable to this book. Thanks also to Dr. Ira Sacker of the Eating Disorders Program at The Brookdale University Hospital and Medical Center, Brooklyn, New York, for his expert reading of the manuscript and Domenica Di Piazza of the Hazelden Foundation for her editorial comments.

Poem appearing on pp. 6–7 reprinted with permission of Patricia Kositzky.

The people pictured in this book are only models. They in no way practice or endorse the activities illustrated. Captions serve only to explain the subjects of photographs and do not in any way imply a connection between the real-life models and the staged situations. News agency photos are exceptions.

Published in 1999 by the Rosen Publishing Group, Inc.
29 East 21st Street, New York, NY 10010

**Library of Congress Cataloging-in-Publication Data**

Smith, Erica.
Anorexia Nervosa : when food is the enemy / Erica Smith.
       p.    cm. — (Teen health library of eating disorder prevention)
Includes bibliographical references and index.
Summary: Describes the origins and symptoms of anorexia nervosa, who is at risk, why it develops in certain individuals, and how it can be prevented and treated.
ISBN 0-8239-2766-0
1. Anorexia Nervosa—Juvenile literature. [1. Anorexia Nervosa.]
  I. Title. II. Series.
RC552.A5S6 1998
616.85′262—dc21
                                            98-29713
                                              CIP
                                              AC

*Manufactured in the United States of America*

# Contents

# Preface: The Girl

*the girl*
*black dress the*
*smallest size hanging*
*positively off her bones*
*at the angle of deprivation*
*a special and serious triangle*
*she is 11 years old or so*
*and Cyndy my friend spots her*
*out immediately*
*anorexic she says*
*lookit her legs*
*and i do my breath*
*gets sharp*
*as her knees*
*no she's too young*
*no she's not*

*she's wearing banana nail polish*
*she knows what's what*
*she totters like*
*an old and wasted woman*
*oh and devours cups of fruit*
*i've had 14 cups of fruit today*
*she says proud amazed and*
*i break inside Cyndy vows*
*to begin a career in counseling*
*don't kill yourself we*
*whisper incantations*
*over our brie and bread*

—Patricia Kositzky

# Introduction

This book is about an eating disorder called anorexia nervosa, commonly called anorexia. You may have heard the term used before—maybe you talked about it in health class, read about it in a magazine, or heard someone talk about how 1970s' pop singer Karen Carpenter died from it. Your mom may get upset if you don't want to finish your dinner and say, "Please eat! You're not becoming ANOREXIC, are you?"

Chances are, eating-related issues probably influence your life right now. As a teen, you might already feel the forces that cause an eating disorder to kick in: insecurity, peer pressure, and society's pressure to be thin.

The word *anorexia* literally means "loss of appetite." But anorexia is more like self-starvation—when someone becomes so obsessed with losing weight and dieting that he or she ignores the body's hunger signals. Although a person with anorexia is always hungry, he or she takes pride in denying hunger, feeling more in control and independent. This belief has very dangerous consequences. If anorexia progresses far enough, a person loses massive amounts of body weight—enough to cause physical problems and even death.

Anorexia is a deadly illness. But unlike flu, or a sexually transmitted disease (STD), anorexia isn't spread by bacteria or a virus. Instead, anorexia arises from your thoughts and emotions.

Currently, more than 8 million Americans suffer from eating disorders. Ninety to 95 percent of those who suffer are female, and the number of males with eating disorders is increasing.

Researchers are slowly beginning to better understand anorexia. But it can only be prevented and conquered when a person can confront the emotions that cause and fuel it.

In this book, you'll read about the causes of anorexia and its signs and symptoms. You may be struggling with anorexia, or someone you know may be suffering from it. This book can help you understand what's going on. It also will point you to resources that will help you change anorexia's destructive course.

# Anorexia Is an Eating Disorder

*"I eat a lot. I have to! I play basketball every day and I need energy."*

*"We don't eat dinner together at my house anymore. It's like no one cares. Either I make a peanut butter sandwich or I don't eat at all."*

*"I hate dinnertime. My mom and dad are always telling me to eat more. So what if I don't eat as much as they do! They tell me I'm anorexic, but it's none of their business."*

How do you feel about food? You probably don't have a simple answer.

We need food in order to survive and grow. But eating also has emotional and social importance for everyone. It's how we bond with each other on holidays, at the movies, at home. And sometimes there are expectations, even pressures, surrounding what and how much we eat.

If you have a healthy relationship with food, you're able to eat when you are hungry and enjoy what you eat. But sometimes food and eating cause discomfort, guilt, conflicts with others, and even self-hatred.

An eating disorder arises when these negative feelings about food become overwhelming and interfere with your health and nutrition. Your eating becomes "disordered," causing both physical and emotional troubles.

## Anorexia: The Basics

As an eating disorder, anorexia nervosa is complicated as well as dangerous. A person with anorexia:

- has an intense fear of gaining weight
- refuses to eat enough to get adequate nutrition
- loses at least 15 percent of his or her body weight

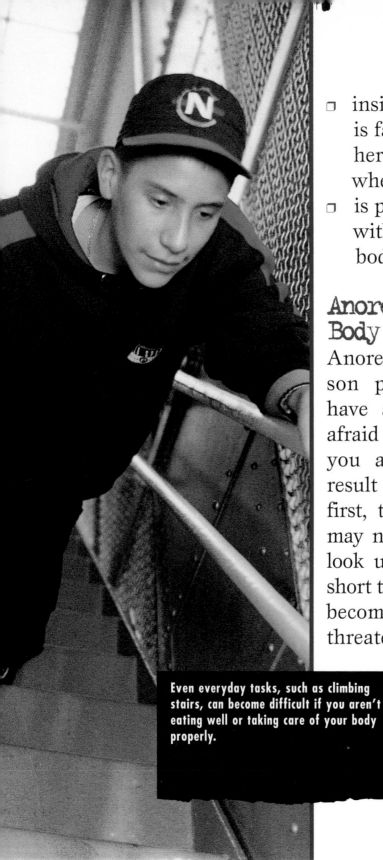

- insists that there is fat on his or her body, even when none exists
- is preoccupied with his or her body image

## Anorexia and the Body

Anorexia affects a person physically. If you have anorexia, you are afraid of getting fat, so you avoid eating. The result is weight loss. At first, the drop in weight may not be noticeable or look unhealthy. But in a short time, the weight loss becomes dramatic and threatens your mental and physical health.

Even everyday tasks, such as climbing stairs, can become difficult if you aren't eating well or taking care of your body properly.

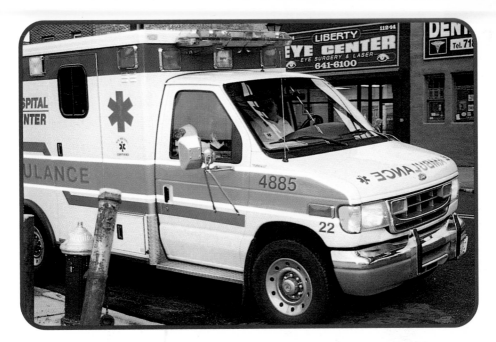

Eating disorders such as anorexia have such a negative impact on your physical well-being that you may need emergency medical attention.

*"At my worst . . . I fainted nearly every day. The anorexia stopped my period for two years. I was taking laxatives regularly because I was constipated. But I used them so much I couldn't control my bowel movements at all."*

Anorexia affects all of your body functions. As the disorder progresses, your digestion slows down and you become constipated. You're always cold because you've lost the protective layer of fat that insulates you. Fine hair, called lanugo, grows all over your body. If you're female, your menstrual period stops. You also will look and feel tired, have a pasty complexion, feel weak, lose your hair, and have fainting spells and headaches. The soles of your palms and feet turn yellow because your body is lacking many of the nutrients it needs to function properly.

When you aren't getting enough nutrition from food, your body will start to break down muscles in order to produce energy. Your liver and kidneys are damaged from this stress, leading to kidney failure. This can be fatal, or require you to be on dialysis for the rest of your life.

Anorexia may make females infertile, or unable to have children, because fertility depends on having a certain amount of body fat. You also may develop osteoporosis—a condition in which your bones become brittle and may even break.

Your heart can be especially affected. Anorexia disturbs the mineral balance in your body,

**The long-term effects of anorexia nervosa can be emotionally devastating as well as deadly.**

which can cause cardiac arrest and death.

## Anorexia and Emotions

Anorexia often begins because of emotional reasons. People who suffer from eating disorders are trying to use food as a way to fill emotional needs, such as love and belonging, or to ease loneliness.

Yet anorexia actually worsens a painful emotional cycle. You become stressed out when you're around food because you feel tempted to eat. And if you do eat, you feel defeat and regret—you may even hate yourself. These feelings become so overwhelming, it's common for depression to set in.

Anorexia makes it hard for you to think and perceive things normally. When your body isn't getting the nutrients it needs, you run on adrenaline (a hormone that kicks in when you're fearful or stressed) instead of on energy from food. These chemical changes affect your personality. You have wider mood swings and a quicker temper.

Also, the more weight you lose, the more distorted your body image becomes. You see fat on your body when you really are dangerously thin.

# Other Eating Disorders

If you have anorexia, chances are you've also had a bout with another eating disorder. Besides anorexia, the most common eating disorders are bulimia nervosa and compulsive eating (also called binge-eating disorder). Eating disorder experts estimate that almost 50 percent of people with anorexia also have struggled with another eating disorder at some time.

## Bulimia Nervosa

When someone suffers from bulimia nervosa or bulimia, he or she binges (or uncontrollably eats a large quantity of food in a short time) and purges (or eliminates the food, usually by vomiting, using laxatives, or taking diuretics, also known as water pills). Bulimia also does

People suffering from anorexia or another eating disorder, such as bulimia nervosa, may resort to taking over-the-counter diet drugs or laxatives.

major damage to the body. It can cause ulcers (holes or tears) in the stomach, throat, and mouth. People with bulimia can develop yellow, damaged teeth from the acids bought up into the mouth through repeated vomiting. Abusing laxatives causes painful stomach cramps and weakens the digestive system.

## Compulsive Eating

Compulsive eating is a disorder in which a person eats uncontrollably but doesn't purge afterward. People with compulsive eating disorder eat large amounts of food very quickly whether or not they feel hungry. They usually do this in private and feel unable to control how much or what they eat. If a person overeats regularly, he or she may forget how to read the body's normal hunger signals and not know how to satisfy them.

## Other Eating-Related Problems

Other problems—compulsive exercise and abuse of medicines and drugs—also accompany eating disorders. Compulsive exercise is an unhealthy drive to over-exercise in order to burn calories and stay thin. This may mean running dozens of miles a day or vowing to do twenty sit-ups for every bite of food you take. Compulsive exercise puts stress on your organs and joints, causing stress fractures and torn muscles.

People with eating-related problems may also abuse medicines and drugs. This includes taking appetite suppressants (drugs that speed up your metabolism), diuretics (drugs that make your body lose water through frequent urination), laxatives (drugs that bring on a bowel movement), and drugs to induce vomiting.

By forcing food and water out of your body, you are upsetting your body's normal functions. Abusing laxatives can cause you to lose control over your bowels. When a person stops using laxatives, the body becomes swollen from retaining water. Other over-the-counter diet drugs can help bring on mineral imbalances that lead to heart failure.

## Who Gets Anorexia?

Anyone can get anorexia—male or female, young or old, and from all walks of life. However, anorexia is much more common in teens than in adults. It seldom sets in after age twenty-five. There also is a higher rate of anorexia among females than among males. This may be because society puts much more pressure on young women than on young men to be thin. Also, since anorexia is thought of mainly as a woman's problem, men may be too shy to seek help, and may, therefore, be underrepresented in the statistics.

Because not all people with an eating disorder seek help, no one is sure exactly how many people suffer from anorexia. But it's estimated that 1 in 250 young women between the ages of twelve and eighteen have struggled with an eating disorder at some time. And five to ten percent of those who struggle with long-term anorexia die from it—the highest death rate of any emotional problem.

# The Beginnings of Anorexia

2

Think of anorexia as a forest fire. You need to have all the right conditions in order for it to start. But if the conditions are right, all it needs is one spark to set it off. And once it starts, it spreads fast until it's out of control.

*I remember exactly when the anorexia started. I was with the school nurse because I got my period unexpectedly and needed a tampon. I was four-teen, but I got my first period when I was ten. I was very self-conscious. Here I was in middle school, but I was taller than almost everyone else and had what my mom called a very "womanly" body.*

*As I was about to leave, the nurse asked me if I had gone to my primary care doctor yet for my yearly checkup. When I said no, she said, "You may want to go, Kim, to keep an eye on yourself. You don't want to gain too much weight." I thought I would die on the spot. I decided right then I had to go on a diet, no matter what. Little did I know that I wouldn't be able to stop dieting once I started.*

Anorexia can be sparked in many ways. As in Kim's case, it can start as a diet—a resolution to shed five or ten pounds—that soon gets out of control.

The amount of stress in your life can play a role in the onset of anorexia. Anorexia is more likely to set in during a time of crisis or transition, such as reaching puberty, going to college, breaking up with someone, or having family problems.

There are many other factors that help set the stage for anorexia, too, and you'll read about them in this chapter. It's important to know as much as you can about how eating disorders take hold so you can keep yourself from falling into dangerous patterns.

# Society's Impact

Our society places a high value on thinness. In fact, many people believe that in order to be beautiful, you *have* to be thin.

When the media—television, movies, and advertising—widely promote this ideal, it becomes difficult to ignore. And it affects what you think is normal. You may start to think that all people are supposed to look as thin as actors and models, when in fact very few people in the world are that thin.

This ideal also affects your feelings about yourself. You may think that losing weight will make you feel more

Looking at idealized images of beauty can make even the healthiest, most well-adjusted people feel insecure about their bodies and their looks.

beautiful, loved, accepted, or popular. But trying to be that thin is unhealthy and impossible for most people.

## Thin Wasn't Always In

Even though thin is popular now, that wasn't always the case. From thousands of years ago up until the mid 1960s, the ideal woman was shapely and soft. Women with full figures were considered desirable because they represented fertility, sexuality, and wealth.

You can see this ideal in the art of many societies. Often, goddesses were portrayed with curvy breasts, stomachs, and buttocks. You also can see this ideal of the female body in the Renaissance paintings of Peter Paul Rubens (this is why full-figured women sometimes are called Rubenesque).

This ideal of the female body held true for a long time. But somewhere along the way, ideas changed. And they have had dramatic effects on American society even very recently.

For example, during the 1950s and 1960s, Marilyn Monroe was one of America's most popular sex symbols. She had a beautiful, voluptuous body. But did you know that if Marilyn were modeling today, she would wear a size 16? That size is hard to find in today's most popular stores, much less on women in television, movies, modeling, or advertising!

The thin-ideal has continued to go to the extreme. One example of this change is the heroin chic look of the 1990s. Models (both male and female) with very thin bodies and dark circles under their eyes became the ultimate statement of what's cool and sexy. But they looked a lot less healthy and radiant than Marilyn or the goddesses of ancient art.

## What's Wrong with Thin Being In?

Placing too much value on thinness has had negative consequences, especially for teenage girls. It can lead you to become anti-fat—cutting all fat out of your diet and trying to eliminate it from your body. And that can lead to unhealthy dieting and anorexia, which interrupt how you're supposed to grow.

People need to eat healthy foods in order to take care of their bodies. And as a teen, you need to eat even more than other people because your body is still growing and changing.

Another problem with wanting to be thin is that most people are not naturally thin. All bodies look different and grow at different rates. Genetics (the

Marilyn Monroe would be considered heavy by today's standards.

traits inherited from your mother and father) play a major role in deciding what body shape you will have, just as they determine the color of your hair and your eyes.

If you have set an unrealistic goal about how you want to look, you will feel disappointed when you cannot attain it. This can cause the depression that contributes to the onset of eating disorders.

## Your Emotions Play a Part

*Josh was fifteen when his mom died of leukemia. She had been sick for more than a year, and in the past six months, Josh and his family knew that nothing more could be done for her. Still, when his mom died,*

**Your parents' physical characteristics help determine your physical characteristics, including body type.**

*Josh was shocked. He didn't know what to feel—grief, anger, or relief that his mother's pain had ended and he could go on with his life. Josh even surprised himself when he didn't cry at the funeral.*

*Some of Josh's friends came to the house when the family was sitting shivah. Hanging out in Josh's bedroom, Tom said, "I'm thinking about trying out for the cross-country team next week. Want to do it with me?"*

*"Sure," Josh shrugged, not really caring what he was going to do in the future.*

*But Tom held him to it and brought Josh to practice. The first two weeks of running were really rough. But soon Josh could feel his body getting stronger. He liked it when his muscles were sore. Soon Josh's friends, and even his dad, were commenting on how good he looked. What's more, Josh felt as if he were proving that he was bouncing back from his mother's death and didn't need anyone's sympathy.*

*Josh got so involved with his running, it soon became the only thing he thought about. Even after coming home from practice and eating dinner, Josh would run a few miles. Soon Josh stopped eating dinner. And lunch. He went running right after he came home from school until the sun went down.*

It's true that anorexia has deep roots in the values and ideals of society. But it also has a lot to do with your emotions. Often, anorexia sets in when you can't put your feelings into words or openly handle what's bothering you.

In Josh's case, he started running as a way to cope with his mother's death. But Josh's efforts soon got out of hand and put him on the path to anorexia. With anorexia, losing weight becomes an obsession—a very intense, persistent thought that you can't block out.

## Control Is an Issue

Often, people with anorexia will view not eating or compulsive exercising as solutions to problems, vowing to lose another five pounds when they feel upset or stressed out. They try to control their bodies by denying food when they can't control what is happening around them.

This is especially true if many things in your life feel beyond your control. In Josh's case, he had just lost his mother. If you aren't allowed to make decisions for yourself or have suffered physical or verbal abuse, you may turn to dieting and exercise as ways to find control in your life.

*"My mom was an alcoholic. You never knew what she was going to be like—screaming one day, apologizing the next. I was so angry with her, I couldn't handle it. I just stopped eating. I felt it would make me rise above the problem. But by the time I got down to 85 pounds, I had even more problems than I did when I started."*

Using anorexia as a way to find control quickly becomes self-destructive. As anorexia sets in, it starts to control you. Soon all of your thoughts and actions revolve around food and eating rather than the emotions you are feeling.

If you feel out of control in your life, it is important to ask for help. Sometimes that just means telling people how you feel. For example, if your parents make family decisions without asking your opinion, you can tell them that you want to be more involved. Then you can work on a plan to keep you in the decision-making loop.

However, if you are in an abusive situation, you need to take strong action. Tell an adult you trust that you need help. He or she will help you find a way to be safe.

## Messages from Friends and Family

*Ella was so excited that she finally had friends to hang around with. She was worried when she changed schools mid-year and thought that she'd never fit in. Now, not only did she have friends, but they were some of the most popular girls in her grade. Ella, Sarah, and Diana had fifth-period lunch together.*

*"Ugh, I just can't eat anything today," Diana sighed as she pushed away her lunch bag. "My mom made cheese-cake last night and I had a piece. I feel fat and disgusting."*

*"Oh, I know," Sarah said. "My thighs are just out of control. No lunch for me, either."*

*Ella stopped eating her peanut butter sandwich mid-bite. If Sarah thought she was fat, what did she think of her? Ella looked down at her own thighs. Maybe I should go on a diet, she thought.*

Having friends is important for teens. You want to fit in and be accepted. But fitting in can mean feeling pressure to dress, look, and act in a way that reinforces the problems that lead to eating disorders. Many people—girls especially—will bond through "fat talk," or sympathizing over how fat they think they look and how much they hate their bodies. As a group, you may be bringing each other down.

Like your friends, family members may indulge in fat talk. It isn't uncommon for parents and kids to go on diets together—even when the son or daughter hasn't hit puberty yet.

Sometimes parents may directly criticize you for what you look like or how much you eat. This may be intended as concern for your social life and goals—"If you keep eating desserts every night, you'll never find a prom date." But it does more harm than

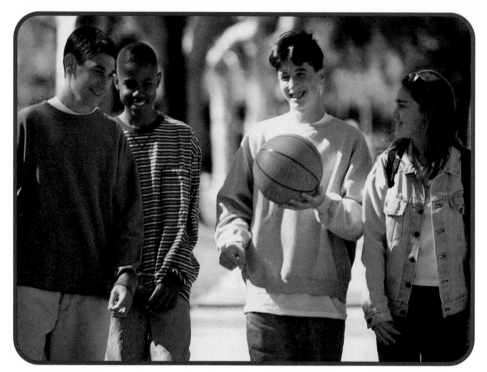

Your friends' positive attitudes about their own bodies, eating habits, and physical activities can help you view your own body in a more positive way.

good. The message comes across that you're not good enough the way you are.

These kinds of negative comments can set up a battlefield mentality between you and your parents. By commenting on your food intake, your parents come across as criticizing—even controlling—you. And you may respond by defying them.

Sometimes a teen will purposely overeat in order to enrage his or her thin-conscious parents. Other times, a teen will fall into anorexic patterns, thinking that being thinner will bring approval or that starvation will bring attention. But these are unhealthy ways to cope with the problem.

It's possible to speak up against the anti-fat mentality. When you're a teen and want to be accepted by others, it may be hard to believe that weight does not matter. But there are things that matter more—like finding out who you are inside, setting and meeting goals, and tapping into the energy inside of you. If people around you make a big deal about weight, you don't have to go along with it.

*"My boyfriend seemed to be commenting on my weight a lot. I started to get very depressed about it, checking myself in the mirror all the time. Finally I told him how much it bugged me. He responded by saying that he didn't want a girlfriend with a big butt! I couldn't believe it! Needless to say, that was the end of the relationship."*

*"When my friends start talking about how they hate this or that body part, I tell them to quit it. Big deal if we have cellulite on our thighs! We should just learn to like ourselves."*

Your attitudes about yourself can bring on or prevent an eating disorder. In the next chapter, you can look at yourself—your emotions, attitudes, and habits—to see where you fit on the self-esteem scale.

By improving your self-esteem, you can take a giant step toward preventing anorexia.

# Am I at Risk?

What makes someone likely to develop an eating disorder? As you can see from everything you've read so far, there is no single cause. Eating disorders are complex problems. They can be fueled by a combination of things, including society's messages, biological and psychological issues, and family issues. Experts study these factors all the time.

Even if you experience problems in one or more of these

areas, it doesn't mean that you automatically will have an eating disorder. The onset of anorexia has a strong link to your self-esteem—your opinion of yourself.

## Self-Perception and the Danger Zones

People who have high self-esteem—a positive view of themselves—have less risk of developing an eating disorder. This means that they value their own ideas and opinions, are eager to try new things, and speak up when something is bothering them.

*"I was really scared to audition for the school musical. I sang in my church choir, but I never had any solos. However, if you consider how I sing along with the radio and dance around the bedroom, I guess you could say I was totally experienced.*

*"When the time came to audition, I was surprised at everything the director wanted us to do. She had us dance—first in a big group, then in groups of four. I had no idea what was going on. So when I forgot a step, I just found my own groove and tried not to let on. My best friend was in the back of the auditorium shouting, 'You go, girl!'*

*"When the time came to sing, it was a little harder to hide my fear. My voice was shaking pretty bad. But thankfully, it was over fast.*

*"As it turns out, I was cast in the chorus. I was a little disappointed that I didn't get a speaking part, but maybe I will next year."*

In comparison, people at risk for anorexia tend to share a less-than-flattering attitude about themselves. They feel misunderstood, think their ideas aren't important, try very hard to be perfect, and shy away from trying new things because they're afraid to fail.

*"I just got pictures back from the ski trip. The trip was really fun. But now that I look at the pictures, I think I look like a cow! No wonder George paid absolutely no attention to me. I was going to ask him out, but forget it. I've got to lose weight."*

If you have low self-esteem, you probably feel that you have little control over what happens to you. You probably also have a hard time believing that you are beautiful. These things may lead you to attempt to achieve the unrealistic "beautiful = thin" ideal.

There are other attitudes that make you vulnerable to anorexia too. Ask yourself the following questions:

*Do you minimize your accomplishments?* This means you don't credit yourself where credit is due. If you score the winning point in a basketball game, you say, "Well, anyone could have done it." If you ace a test, you say, "It wasn't that hard anyway." You miss out on enjoying the positive things you're able to achieve, convinced that you still didn't do well enough.

*Do you not see yourself as others see you?* Other people may see you putting yourself down and tell you that you're better than you give yourself credit for. But you usually discredit what they say by thinking, "Well, she's my mom, of course she thinks I'm great" or "He doesn't know what he's talking about."

*Do you criticize your body?* Any unhappiness and tension that you feel gets directed toward your body. You feel unattractive and imperfect. You think that losing weight will make you feel better about yourself and will make other people like you.

## Change Is Possible

Even if you fit many of the descriptions for low self-esteem, you are not necessarily destined or doomed to develop an eating disorder. It's possible to overcome many of the roadblocks to self-esteem.

# Tips for Prevention

It's possible to change low self-esteem to help prevent an eating disorder from kicking in. Try these preventative measures:

Educate yourself about eating disorders. Know how they start and what they do to you.

Don't go along with fat talk. If your friends are in the habit of putting themselves down and criticizing their bodies, let them know that it bugs you. Be positive. Try saying, "Actually, I like myself. I look just like my aunt did at my age, and I think she's so cool. So what if I'm not a size two."

Get involved with sports that emphasize strength (such as basketball and biking) rather than body shape (such as ballet or gymnastics).

Throw out your scale and give away clothes that don't fit. Save up some money to buy clothes that feel comfortable. When you're comfortable and relaxed, your fabulous inner self will shine through.

Think critically about the advertising you see. If you're sick of magazines showing only waiflike models, let the editors of those magazines know. You can pressure them by saying you won't buy their publications anymore.

Express your feelings. Your opinions count. If you're hurt or upset, say so. It's better to agree to disagree than to keep your true feelings inside.

Seek help when you feel out of control. Talk to a trusted adult (family member, doctor, counselor) and always remember that you are not alone. There is help available when and if you need it.

Stay in touch with your feelings and what's going on in your life. Express yourself and don't be afraid to ask for help when you need it. You can use your self-knowledge to keep from falling into the patterns that lead to a full-blown eating disorder. This can mean: finding friends who don't make a big deal out of food and body size; writing down your thoughts (taping them on a portable tape recorder works too); getting involved with sports, hobbies, or youth groups; and/or getting help by talking with a therapist, counselor, or school social worker.

In the next chapter, you'll see why it's so important to have a strong and positive self-image. Anorexia is an illness that can start very innocently but grow until it consumes most of your energy. It keeps you from becoming the best you can be.

# The Quest for Thinness

Anorexia never happens overnight or for any one reason. When a person develops anorexia, he or she doesn't necessarily make a conscious choice to put his or her health and life in jeopardy. Instead, the anorexia is a response to, or way of coping with, the roadblocks to self-esteem. It gives you something to focus on other than the unhappiness or tension you feel inside. But soon anorexia starts to create its own kind of tension.

## In the Beginning

As you know, anorexia often starts as a diet. But the more weight you lose, the more you want to lose.

One of the first signs of

anorexia is that you make your diet regimen more and more strict. This means making what seem to be sensible choices at first—cutting out all red meat, skipping dessert, and choosing low-fat or nonfat alternatives to foods such as cream cheese and salad dressing. You soon begin restricting your intake of other foods, too, limiting yourself to white meat and vegetables and reducing the size of your portions.

In the beginning, you may even receive admiration and praise as you start to lose weight. The attention feels good. But privately, you feel that you still need to lose more weight. You may exercise for long periods of time in order to make sure that you keep losing weight and don't level off.

## You're in Jeopardy

Soon shedding pounds becomes the most important thing in your life—the yardstick by which you measure and judge yourself. You may start checking yourself in the mirror and weighing yourself several times a day. Your moods are deeply affected by what you see. You're relieved if the scale shows weight loss and devastated if it shows a gain.

Other aspects of your self-perception have changed, too. When you look at your body, you see yourself more as a set of body parts—hips, thighs, stomach—than as a whole person. You become rigid in your thinking, vowing to elminate pounds

While it's okay to know how much you weigh, it is harmful to become preoccupied with your weight. You don't need to weigh yourself several times a day.

in the areas you don't like on your body. You think of losing weight as a positive action, not realizing that this intense scrutiny is actually harming your self-esteem.

## The Importance of Rituals

Rituals are an important ingredient in the development of anorexia. Often, rituals center around mealtimes. You may devise a rigid plan in which you eat different foods, cut the food up into tiny pieces, and chew a certain number of times before you swallow.

It's also common to inspect your food intensely, checking for anything that looks funny. If you find something you can't identify, you feel justified in rejecting the meal. To a healthy person, your actions appear more and more irrational.

*"I wasn't a whole lot of fun when I had anorexia. I was terrified to go anywhere there might be food. I was always worrying about rules and judging people. My friends were very freaked out by this change in me. I was a shell."*

## Tuning Out

As you continue to deny yourself food and force yourself to maintain rituals, your normal self shuts down even more. Being hungry all the time alters your personality.

*"I felt very isolated because most of the people I knew did not understand what I was going through. They were very frustrated and aggravated. People tried, but I was difficult*

Denying your body nutrients will affect not only your physical performance but also your mood.

*to be around. I pushed them away."*

One typical change in behavior is that you grow more impatient with others. You become more focused on yourself. You withdraw from friends and family by not going out or returning phone calls. People around you may express serious concern about your extreme weight loss, but you're convinced that they are trying to sabotage you. You feel that the anorexia gives you a sense of power and invincibility.

By the time you reach this stage, you have a full-blown case of anorexia. You will show these physical signs of illness:

- ❑ weight loss of 15 percent below normal weight
- ❑ fatigue or hyperactivity
- ❑ irregular or absent menstrual periods
- ❑ muscle weakness
- ❑ dizziness and/or fainting
- ❑ skin problems
- ❑ always being cold

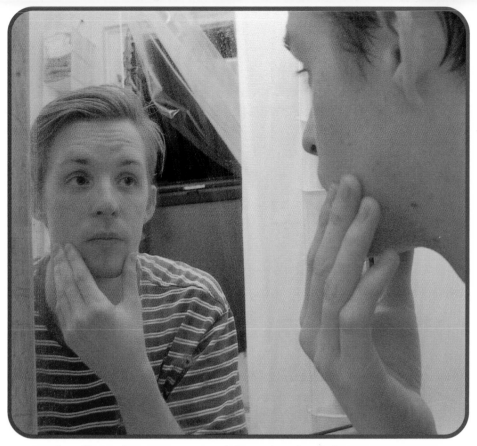

People suffering from anorexia may believe that their behavior is improving how they look. But symptoms such as breakouts or bloating show otherwise.

- ❐ constipation
- ❐ yellow palms and soles
- ❐ loss of hair from scalp
- ❐ growth of fine, downy hair on the body
- ❐ insomnia
- ❐ bloating
- ❐ dehydration
- ❐ loss of sexual feelings

When you experience these symptoms of anorexia, you are doing major harm to your body. Although you

Anorexia nervosa can isolate you from friends and family when you most need their support and help.

still believe that the anorexia is making you powerful and in control, you probably feel scared and lonely underneath.

This loneliness may become worse as the illness progresses. You may get into more fights with family, or even worse, watch family members fight about (or over) you. People may start to relate to you differently, alternately babying, arguing with, and avoiding you. You may end up feeling more alienated than you did at the outset.

## Choosing to Stop

If the anorexia continues, you may risk death. Your

organs will start to shut down, and you will have liver, kidney, and heart problems. But it's possible to stop the illness before then. At first, you may not want to stop. Or you may want to but are afraid to do so. It is scary, but that's part of the illness of anorexia. It makes you feel as if it's the only thing that matters, that if you gave up anorexia, you'd be nothing without it.

But the truth is, anorexia is holding you back. It takes up all of your energy—energy you otherwise could spend growing and learning about yourself and living a healthy life.

It is possible to recover with the help of professionals. And once you break the pattern, you'll see new opportunities open to you.

*"Anorexia took a lot of life from me; it took a lot of years. I mean, I had the years still, but I didn't live them to the fullest. It stole a lot of time from me.*

*It's not worth dying for—it definitely isn't worth dying for."*

# Choosing Health

5

*I was flipping channels and started watching a television movie about a woman who died from anorexia. I had been starving myself for about two months. Nobody knew it, but I was sick and unhappy all the time. Watching the movie made me realize I needed help. I knew I had to make up my mind to change right then, or else I would get too scared.*

*The next day I hung around after social studies class. Ms. Dominguez is my favorite teacher, and I knew she had a free period. I asked her if I could talk to her in private. She shut the door and asked what was up.*

*"I've got a big secret," I said. My voice was trembling. "I haven't been eating. And sometimes I make myself throw up. I feel really scared. I don't know what to do." I started crying.*

*I thought Ms. Dominguez would freak out when she heard what I was doing. But she didn't. "Look, it's going to be okay," she said. "I'm glad you told me. Let's think about what we can do."*

Admitting you have an eating disorder is the hardest thing you can do when you have anorexia. People probably have tried to confront you about it before. But sometimes people's concerns can feel like pressures and threats. They may say, "You're tearing this family apart," or "Your father and I don't know what to do with you," or "If you don't eat something, I'm sending you to a therapist."

You probably want—and need—people's love and concern. It's possible that someone may confront you when the time is right and you're ready to take him or her up on an offer for help. But, especially if you're taken by surprise or someone doesn't express himself or herself in the best way, you're likely to reject any help that is offered.

Opening up to a family member or close friend can give you the confidence you need to seek professional help and start on the road to recovery.

That's why it's important to take matters into your own hands and choose who to tell and how to say it. The first time you admit to another person that you have a problem can feel very awkward. But if you think it through first, you'll feel more comfortable when the time comes.

## What to Do When You Tell Someone

1) Tell an authority figure. You can tell a friend, too, but it's important to tell someone who has more insight about what to do. This could be your parents or a friend's parents, an older sister or brother,

a teacher, a counselor, or someone from your religious congregation.

2) Pick a time that's good to talk. Make sure you have enough time and a quiet space. Schedule your meeting in advance, even if it's a family meeting.

3) Have a support person with you if you need it. This could be a friend or a professional such as a social worker or therapist who already knows that you have an eating disorder.

4) Think about what you're going to say and how. You don't have to write down a script. But it may help to come up with a few key phrases or points beforehand, such as:

  - ❑ "I know you have brought this up with me before and I denied it. But I have a problem with food. I'm ready to talk about it now."
  - ❑ "I haven't been eating. I need your help."
  - ❑ "I need to bring a problem out in the open. I'm afraid of eating. I need to talk with you about what to do."

5) Be prepared that people's reactions may not be what you expected. Although you have planned

in advance, you may find that the person isn't comfortable handling the information. It may mean that someone gets angry at you, tries to one-up you with a story about him- or herself, or goes on as if nothing has happened. If this happens, you will need to speak to another person who can help you now.

## Therapy

After telling someone, you probably will feel a great sense of relief. You no longer have to deal with anorexia alone. And all the energy that you were putting into your anorexia can now be used to get healthy.

One major aspect of recovery from anorexia is therapy. This is not as scary as it sounds. Essentially, therapy (short for psychotherapy) is talking to a neutral person (a therapist) about what's going on in your life. The more you talk, the more you discover about yourself. When issues come up in your life, you have two heads working on solving them instead of just one.

Therapy is especially helpful for dealing with eating disorders. The better you know yourself, the better equipped you are to build your self-esteem. At the same time, you can work on pinpointing the patterns of thought or the life experiences that brought on the eating disorder and prevent them from happening again.

## What to Do First

A good first step is to visit your primary-care doctor. Even

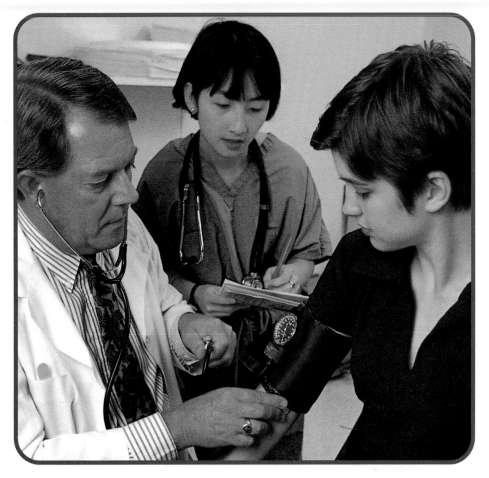

Your doctor can explain treatment options to you and your family. Together you can make an educated decision about your recovery plan.

if you haven't been to the doctor in a while, it's important that he or she knows what's going on. Often your primary physician may refer you to an eating disorder specialist.

If you are covered under an insurance plan, contact your insurance company and find out about its mental health benefits. Your parents or another adult can do this for you, but make sure they tell you what they find out.

It's important to be involved in deciding what your recovery plan will be. Sit down with your primary-care doctor and family and talk about the options that are available. Together you can decide what works best for you, depending on your needs and your family's financial situation.

## Choosing the Right Recovery for You

There will be many recovery routes open to you. It's possible that if you are very ill, you may need to be hospitalized until your medical condition stabilizes. In addition to being treated for any medical problems, you will get psychological and nutritional counseling while you're there. When you're released from the hospital, you'll be able to work out the next phase of your recovery.

Also, an insurance company may arrange for you to meet with a therapist of its choice. You can talk with a company representative about the different kinds of therapy available. You will want to think about your preferences—whether or not you want a male or female therapist, for example. You also can decide if you want a short-term or long-term therapy (different therapists use different formats). From there, you will be referred to another person or program.

You may find that a clinic situation will work best for you. Clinics specializing in eating disorders are often free. They may be inpatient, which means you live there while receiving treatment, or outpatient, which means you come in during the day and go home at night. These clinics are especially beneficial because they are designed to treat eating disorders.

There are many different kinds of therapy, which fall under a few major categories. It's probable that, when you are recovering, you'll have a team of people helping you.

- Individual therapy: You meet with a therapist one-on-one. A therapist may be a psychologist (therapist with a Ph.D.), a psychiatrist (a psychologist who also is a medical doctor), or a licensed social worker.

- Family therapy: You and your family meet with a therapist. This helps your family learn more about eating disorders and how to help you.

- Group therapy: You meet with a group of people who share the same type of problem and, together with a therapist, discuss solutions.

- Self-help: You meet with other people who are recovering from eating disorders to share insights. Unlike other avenues to recovery, self-help is not led by a therapist. Members of a group form networks with each other. Self-help also is free.

- Dietitian: Usually together with another kind of therapy, you meet with a dietitian to develop healthy eating habits.

*"I feel stronger, like I can handle my negative feelings. I may choose to confront people about them or not. But that's my choice."*

## Stay Involved

No matter what kind of therapy you choose, it's important to stay involved in the decision-making process. That means asking your therapist about his or her plan for you, and how he or she views the therapy experience. Also, you should know about the training and education he or she has received so you know what to expect from him or her.

You also may want to ask whether your treatment may include medication. This often is hard for a therapist or doctor to tell in advance, but it helps to know where your

> **Fact**
> Antidepressants used to treat eating disorders include Elavil, Nardil, Marplan, Parnate, Prozac, Sinequan, Tofranil, Paxil, and Zoloft.

doctor and therapist stand on the issue. Because experts have found a connection between eating disorders and depression, antidepressants such as Prozac have been used to treat eating disorders. If you are given a prescription, ask your doctor and therapist about the drug and its side effects. You also have the right to request a change in your medication if you feel it is not working.

Staying involved with your progress also is important so you can have a hand in how your therapy is going. Whatever kind of therapy you choose, it is important to find a person you trust. Some therapists spend much of the time listening. Others are much more directive. It's important to express what you like or dislike.

When you're in recovery, it's often hard to get a handle on all the feelings and changes that come up. Some of what you feel will be uncomfortable—that's normal.

# Tips on Confronting Someone You Suspect Has an Eating Disorder

One of the hardest things you can do is confront someone you think is suffering from anorexia. Below are some tips that may help.

Educate yourself about the problem. Read up on eating disorders and talk to a therapist or counselor for information.

Find a time that's good to talk. Wait until you have a quiet time together. Don't confront someone during a tense moment at the dinner table.

Use "I" statements instead of "you" statements. This means approaching someone not to accuse but to let him or her know gently that his or her illness is noticeable and has affected you. Examples: "I noticed you haven't been eating. Is something wrong?" This opens up a dialogue more effectively than simply saying, "You look sick."

Listen to what the person has to say, withholding comments about yourself and your own struggles for the time being.

Be prepared that your help may not be taken. It's important to let someone know you care about him or her. But if he or she isn't ready to change, you cannot force your friend to change.

Be available if your friend needs to reach out to you in the future.

When you can work through these tough emotions, you're actually making progress and becoming more self-aware.

## Setbacks and Gains

Yet it's possible that you may be in a treatment plan that isn't working so well for you. Or you may want to give it all up and go back to anorectic patterns. Don't give up! You already have made the choice for health.

Remember that there are many routes toward recovery. If you can speak up about how you feel, you can work together with others to decide what to do. There are many different approaches for treating anorexia. Sometimes it takes time before you find the right one. Recovery from anorexia is one of the hardest things you will ever do—but it's worth it.

# Glossary

**appetite suppressant** A drug or chemical that reduces hunger/appetite and keeps you from wanting as much food.

**bingeing** Eating large amounts of food in one sitting.

**body image** The way you perceive your body and how you think others perceive your body.

**bulimia** An eating disorder in which someone eats a lot and then purges the food.

**cardiac arrest** When your heart stops beating.

**constipation** Difficulty having bowel movements.

**disordered** Something that doesn't function in the usual way.

**diuretic** A drug that causes an increase in the amount of urine the kidneys produce.

**infertility** The inability to have children.

**laxative**  A drug or substance that brings on a bowel movement.

**nutrition**  Eating a healthy selection of foods in the amounts necessary to maintain health.

**osteoporosis**  A condition that causes bones to become fragile.

**purge**  To rid the body of food, usually through vomiting, exercise, or laxatives.

**ulcers**  Tears or holes in the lining of the stomach, throat, or mouth.

# Where to Go for Help

**American Anorexia/Bulimia Association, Inc. (AABA)**
165 West 46th Street, Suite 1108
New York, NY 10036
(212) 575-6200
Web site: http://members.aol.com/AMANBU

**Anorexia Nervosa and Related Eating Disorders, Inc. (ANRED)**
P. O. Box 5102
Eugene, OR 97405
(541) 344-1144
Web site: http://www.anred.com

**Eating Disorders Awareness and Prevention, Inc. (EDAP)**
603 Stewart Street, Suite 803
Seattle, WA 98101
(206) 382-3587
Web site: http://members.aol.com/edapinc

**Helping to End Eating Disorders (HEED)**
9620 Church Avenue
Brooklyn, NY 11212

(718) 240-6451
Web site: http://www.eatingdis.com

## National Association of Anorexia Nervosa and Associated Disorders (ANAD)

P.O. Box 7
Highland Park, IL 60035
(847) 831-3438
Web site:
http://members.aol.com/anad20/index.html

## National Eating Disorders Organization (NEDO)

6655 South Yale Avenue
Tulsa, OK 74136
(918) 481-4044
Web site: http://www.laureate.com

## In Canada

## Anorexia Nervosa and Associated Disorders (ANAD)

109-2040 West 12th Avenue
Vancouver, BC V6J 2G2
(604) 739-2070

## National Eating Disorder Information Centre

College Wing, 1st Floor, Room 211
200 Elizabeth Street
Toronto, ON M5G 2C4
(416) 340-4156

# For Further Reading

Cooke, Kaz. *Real Gorgeous: The Truth About Body and Beauty.* New York: W. W. Norton, 1996.

Hornbacher, Marya. *Wasted: A Memoir of Anorexia and Bulimia.* New York: HarperCollins, 1998.

Jukes, Mavis. *It's a Girl Thing: How to Stay Healthy, Safe, and in Charge.* New York: Knopf, 1996.

Kolodny, Nancy. *When Food's a Foe: How You Can Confront and Conquer Your Eating Disorder*, rev. ed. Boston: Little, Brown & Co., 1992.

Madaras, Lynda, and Area Madaras. *My Body, My Self for Boys: The 'What's Happening to My Body' Workbook for Boys.* New York: Newmarket Press, 1995.

Madaras, Lynda, and Area Madaras. *My Body, My Self for Girls: The 'What's Happening to My Body' Workbook for Girls.* New York: Newmarket Press, 1993.

McCoy, Kathy, and Charles Wibbelsman, MD. *Life Happens: A Teenager's Guide to Friends, Failure, Sexuality, Love....* New York: Berkley, 1996.

Sacker, Ira, M.D., and Marc A. Zimmer, Ph.D. *Dying to Be Thin: Understanding and Defeating Anorexia Nervosa and Bulimia.* New York: Warner Books, 1987.

# Index

## About the Author

Erica Smith is an editor who has taught writing to children, teens, and adults. She lives in Brooklyn, New York, where she writes, sings, and plays her guitar. She is finally learning to love her body.

**Design and Layout:** Christine Innamorato

**Consulting Editor:** Michele I. Drohan

**Photo Credits:**
Photo on pp. 10, 38, 48 by Skjold Photographs; pp. 12 by John Bentham; p. 13, 14, 22, 25 by Ira Fox; pp. 16, 43 by Maike Schulz; p. 20 © Ron Chapple/FPG International; p. 24 © UPI-Corbis-Bettman; p. 30 © Ken Chernus/FPG International; p. 32 © Tony Anderson/FPG International; p. 44 by John Bentham; p. 40 by Sally Weigand; p. 41 by Kim Sonsky; p. 42 © Tony Demin/International Stock; p. 46 © Barry Rosenthal/FPG International; p. 51 © Michael Paras/International Stock.